WHO YOUR PARACHUTE?

Practical Advice
From The
Chronically Unemployed

by TONY "X" and DANNY "Y"

BAD
DOG
PRESS
™

Bad Dog Press
P.O. Box 130066, Roseville, MN 55113

e-mail: badogpress@aol.com & badogbook@aol.com

Who Packed Your Parachute?
Practical Advice from the Chronically Unemployed.

First printed in 1996

Printed in the United States of America.

96 97 98 99 00   5 4 3 2 1

Text: Tony Dierckins and Danny Naslund
Illustrations: Tim Nyberg

ISBN 1-887317-00-7
Library of Congress Catalog Card Number: 95-83148

Warning: Contains humor, a highly volatile substance if used improperly. Harmful if swallowed. All content is a fictional product of the authors' imaginations. Any resemblance between characters portrayed herein and actual persons living, dead, or residing in New Jersey is purely coincidental. Contents under pressure. Do not use near open flame. Do not use as a flotation device, or at least avoid any situations in which you would need to rely on a book as a flotation device. Any typographic errors are purely intentional and left for your amusement. Always say no to drugs and, by all means, stay in school.

To our family, friends, colleagues past and
present, former teachers and mentors,
and, of course, our patient wives—
all those who once held high
hopes for us and saw in us
the promise of success.

Sorry.

CONTENTS

PREFACE

You may have stumbled across this handbook on a shelf laden with similar volumes, all offering advice on how to procure gainful employment or to advance along your chosen career path. The most popular of these books, *What Color Is Your Parachute?*, has sold something like five million copies in twenty-five years. Its publisher claims it sells five thousand copies a month, and it has been translated into seven languages. Wow. It must be a pretty darn good book.

We've never read that book. We don't even know what the title is supposed to mean. You should probably get yourself a copy if you need work as bad as we do.

You'll want a copy of this book, too. It offers advice you won't find in that other "parachute" book or any other title in the career section. Unlike those other books, we don't claim to have any practical advice on what works when searching for a job.

We do, however, know what does *not* work. We've made a lot of mistakes over the years, soiled a lot of perfectly good suits. We hate to see anyone go through what we have. And so we have filled the following pages with bits of information gleaned from years searching for employment—advice based on mistakes we unwittingly made on our résumés, in our cover letters, and during interviews.

Don't make the same errors we have made. Buy, read, and use this book to your advantage.

—Tony X. and Danny Y.

P.S.

"Tony X." and "Danny Y." are not our real names. Our publisher suggested we use pseudo-nyms as our contract guarantees we may never earn back our advance and therefore we will need to continue our job search. We would also like to take this opportunity to apologize to any personnel managers who manage to identify us.

SECTION ONE: GETTING STARTED

CHAPTER ONE: THE RÉSUMÉ

Did you know that donating plasma is not really work experience? It's true! As a job seeker, you should take care to make certain your résumé is free from such subtle mistakes. Besides your cover letter (see Chapter Two), your résumé or *curriculum vita* is

> **DONATING PLASMA IS NOT REALLY WORK EXPERIENCE.**

your first chance to make a good impression on prospective future employers. Taking the time to ensure yours is well written and correctly punctuated and looks nice is simple common sense. There are, however, some things you will *not* want to include on your résumé. Read on for more valuable tips.

RÉSUMÉ MATTERS OF STYLE

Most prospective employers consider dotting your i's with smiley faces "unprofessional"—an important point most résumé writing books simply gloss over or even ignore. They focus on the obvious: A successful résumé both reads well and looks good: list the dates of your employment in the margins, use active verbs when describing your "responsibilities," etc. Few, however, warn against stylistic subtleties that can "trip up" even the most carefully written *vitae.* Here are a few suggestions to keep your application from landing in the "sorry, but…" pile:

- Having your picture appear in a high school yearbook or your name mentioned in a local newspaper's police blotter does not constitute "publication."

- Punctuation: Since no one actually fully understands the proper use of the semicolon, it is best to avoid using it; the appearance of this ambiguous form of punctuation on a résumé (or in a cover letter) may intimidate some personnel managers.

- There is no need to reveal every little detail in your "responsibilities" sections. If you do, remember to use this simple, three-word sentence when necessary: "Never been convicted."★

- Former postal workers: there is no need to add "disgruntled" to your job title.

- "Larceny" need not be capitalized unless used as part of a nickname. In fact, you should avoid the use of "larceny" as well as the following terms:

  - "Twine"
  - "Indicted"
  - "Cleared up"
  - "French fries"
  - "Liberal/fine arts"
  - "Restraining order"
  - "All better now, though"

★Minnesota residents: Don't take for granted that employers really understand the Huber Law or other features of the work release program.

Your Résumé's "Special Skills" Section

Lactose intolerant? Well, that may be good for a "sick day" here and there, but it is *not* a special skill. That doesn't mean you shouldn't include a special skills section on your *vita*. Never underestimate the importance of letting prospective employers know you can operate office equipment, microcomputers, and specific items connected to your area of expertise. However, some talents that set you apart from other candidates should *not* be listed: make sure to list only actual job-related skills. Use the following as a guide:

- There really is no need to include a "fetishes" category.

- Accompany any use of "animal sacrifice" with a full explanation. (Actually, you don't even need to mention religious affiliations.)

- Unless it pertains to the job, employers really don't care to read about your unique approaches to using talcum powder.

- Your conviction-to-acquittal ratio actually reflects your attorney's skills, not your own.

• Employers are generally unimpressed if you throw right but bat left, and any mention of your ability to switch hit may only confuse some personnel managers.

Hold on there, Slick. You might be pretty good with that whip, but is it something your future boss really must know? Your résumé really doesn't need a "fetishes" category.

"Padding" Your Résumé

Have you ever listed your experience in showing fellow employees how to hide cash register mistakes as "Employee Training Supervisor"? Sure. We all have. It's called "padding" your résumé, and most recent college graduates, particularly those with little relevant work experience, often stretch the truth with this technique. Before you choose to pad your application, consider first how difficult it is to explain anything involving farm animals. And always be careful; you'd be surprised how many personnel managers are aware that the following jobs do not exist:

- "Senior Marketing Director, Entertainment Division."

  Spent a week telling everyone on campus that you and your roommates were going to throw a huge party on the weekend.

- "Advance Reconnaissance Liaison, Brewed Malt Beverages Division"

  Called around to local liquor stores to find the cheapest price on kegs.

College prepared you for a successful career, right? Careful!
Not every extracurricular activity translates well on paper.

- "Purchase Procurement Coordinator, Brewed Malt Beverages Division"

  Found somebody with a truck and a couple guys from the wrestling team to help you get the kegs from the liquor store and carry them into your basement.

- "Treasurer, Entertainment Division"

  Ponied up beer money from your room-mates and sold plastics cups at the door.

- "Custodial Evaluation Consultant"

  Spent the next morning arguing with room-mates over who should clean up the plastic cups and cigarette butts littering the house.

So you see, while your career counselor proba-bly advised you to participate in as many extracurricular activities as possible, not all of them translate well on paper. Frustrated? Don't be. Remember, unless you "know the right peo-ple" or "have the right connections" or "actually graduated," chances are you're not going to get the job you really want anyhow. What really matters is that you try and that, from time to time, you work somewhere long enough to col-lect Worker's Compensation.

CHAPTER TWO:
THE COVER LETTER

If you, like us, have ever had a cover letter returned scribbled with remarks ranging from "please note that 'proofreader' is not hyphenated" to "I suggest you not use crayon in the future," then you already know the importance of a well-written letter of introduction.

> **AVOID BEGINNING A COVER LETTER WITH "YO, JOBMEISTER!"**

No matter how well you've crafted your résumé, without an equally effective cover letter your *vita* may never be read by prospective employers. Common cover letter tips include keeping letters brief and mentioning skills of yours that match the position's qualifications. Remember: personnel managers are sticklers for detail—they're looking for any little excuse to move your application into the "reject" box and make their job easier. To ensure that your application gets the consideration it deserves, follow the guidelines on the ensuing pages.

GENERAL COVER LETTER TIPS

- Always sign off with "Sincerely." Terms of endearment such as "Love" and "Forever Yours" can easily confuse some personnel managers.

- Groveling is apparently ineffective.

- Never enclose cash (cover yourself: use checks or money orders for all your bribes —you never know when you may need documented evidence).

- Postcards, although a great money saver, are generally ignored and even considered "unprofessional."

- Don't use hotel stationery, not even if you're still using the alias "Howard Johnson."

AVOIDING BAD STARTS TO COVER LETTERS

Maybe you've never begun a cover letter with, "Yo, Jobmeister!" That doesn't make you a better person than us, but it does remind us again of the importance of first impressions. This axiom is a staple of employment-related correspondence. In fact, we have found a letter's first sentence can actually determine a résumé's fate. Therefore, in your quest for employment, think carefully about the very start of your letters. We have compiled a list of opening phrases, often born of desperation, that we have determined to be unsuccessful and perhaps even detrimental in a cover letter. Make an effort to eliminate them from your own.

Dear Sir or Madam:

- I know where you live …
- My psychic friend advised me …
- What about my needs?
- How come…?
- I once held cue cards for the "Mike Douglas" show …

- Perhaps you're not familiar with my JFK assassination theory …
- Do you need a hug?
- Okay, these three nuns walk into a locker room …
- If you caught the last "Jenny Jones" …
- I think my dad knows your uncle's brother's neighbor's sister's …
- Now that I have my license back …
- As the Messiah …

POORLY WRITTEN COVER LETTERS

The letters on the following pages represent a sample of those we wrote early in our job searches—before we knew what *not* to include in a successful cover letter. The names of the companies have been changed because we may be forced to apply at the same firm more than once. We hope reading these will help you get it right the first time. See if you can spot the mistakes!

POORLY WRITTEN COVER LETTER #1

1 January 1996

Personnel Manager
Acme Promotions
Anytown, U.S.A.

Sir or Madam:

I write in response to the opening for an events coordinator at Acme Promotions.

I have enclosed my résumé for your consideration. As you will see, I am highly qualified for this position.

I can explain about the kittens.

Sincerely,

Danny Y.

Dɪᴅ ʏᴏᴜ sᴘᴏᴛ ᴛʜᴇ ᴍɪsᴛᴀᴋᴇ?

Most experienced cover letter writers would omit the line about the kittens. Actually, this error should lead careful job searchers to take another look at their résumé—leave out anything that requires explanation.

Better luck on letter #2!

POORLY WRITTEN COVER LETTER #2

1 January 1996

Personnel Manager
Acme Publishing
Anytown, U.S.A.

Sir or Madam:

I write in response to the opening for a editorial assistant at Acme Publishing.

As my résumé (enclosed) will indicate, I am hihly qualified for this position. I don't care what my references may tell you.

Sincerely,

Tony X.

DID YOU SPOT THE MISTAKE?

If you think the "a" before "editorial" should be "an," you are correct! Sure, this may simply be a typo, but personnel managers may interpret it as a language skills inefficiency. Proofread! Proofread! Proofread!

If you've been reading closely, letter #3 should be an easy one.

POORLY WRITTEN COVER LETTER #3

1 January 1996

Personnel Manager
First Acme Savings and Loan
Anytown, U.S.A.

Sir or Madam:

I write in response to the opening for a bank teller at First Acme Savings and Loan.

As mentioned in your ad, I am an honest, highly motivated, independent worker that can be trusted with the responsibility involved in handling large sums of money.

My résumé is enclosed. (Please note that both prior convictions are currently under appeal.)

Sincerely,

Danny Y.

Did you spot the mistake?

Careful readers will note that mentioning prior convictions breaks the rule of not using the term "indicted" on your résumé. Unless they bring it up, there is no reason for you to mention any incidents involving law enforcement agencies or the judicial system.

Keep going!

POORLY WRITTEN COVER LETTER #4

1 January 1996

Personnel Manager
Acme Manufacturing
Anytown, U.S.A.

Sir or Madam:

Pursuant to your advertisement for an accounts manager, I am enclosing my résumé and three letters of reference.

In anticipation of an interview, I thoroughly researched your company and find it conducive to my employment needs. Unfortunately, during my investigation I ripped my best pants on your security fence.

To whom shall I forward the bill?

Sincerely,

Tony X.

DID YOU SPOT THE MISTAKE?

Right! "am enclosing" is a terrifically weak verb choice. Remember, there are those who say it is always best to use active verbs when you are writing cover letters. Regrettably, we never received a response.

Watch out for letter five—it's a tricky one!

POORLY WRITTEN COVER LETTER #5

1 January 1996

Personnel Manager
Acme Investments
Anytown, U.S.A.

Sir or Madam:

I write in response to the account manager opening with Acme Investments' finance department. Please find enclosed my résumé and references.

Also, please note that although I currently have numerous job opportunities at this time, I will work for Acme for free for the first twelve (12) months.

Sincerely,

Danny Y.

Did you spot the mistake?

Yep! "Currently" and "at this time" are redundant—an obvious, devastating, and calamitous error that stood out as the reason behind the rationality of the decision to ultimately eliminate the application from consideration by the potential employer for the position that was being applied for by the applicant, who was eventually rejected.

Chapter Three:
The Personnel Manager
(or, Know Your Adversary)

Most companies big enough to offer benefits employ a personnel manager—a person hired to maintain records of current employees and help hire new ones. Sometimes called the "human resources manager" (a title coined by personnel managers to make their job seem more important), this person is your initial contact with a potential employer. In other words, before you get a job, you have to get past him or her first.

TWO-THIRDS OF ALL PERSONNEL MANAGERS LIVE ALONE AND OWN AT LEAST TWO CATS.

The personnel manager will examine your cover letter and résumé, scrutinizing your every grammatic use in order to separate your application from the profusion of others. He or she will also conduct your initial (or "screening") interview to see if you're even worth the department manager's time. In short, you must first impress the personnel manager to even get a chance to impress your (here's hoping!) future supervisor or department head.

Through personal observations, we have generated some interesting facts about personnel managers. Here's what you should know:

- Because of their unlimited access to personnel files (and, therefore, salary records), many personnel managers are resented by their fellow employees and often eat lunch alone.

- Most personnel managers hold a B.A. in a liberal arts discipline (84 percent majored in communications—they're "people persons"!)

- "Personnel manager" was *not* the first career choice of more than 98 percent of personnel managers.

- Many (77 percent) personnel managers began their working lives at The Gap.

- Highly developed "critical evaluation" skills have doomed any chance for personnel managers to enjoy happy, normal interpersonal relationships.

- The average personnel manager fills out three graduate school applications each year.

Don't care for personnel managers? You're not the only one. In fact, their overdeveloped critical evaluation skills doom their chances at having normal, healthy relationships.

- Fifty-nine percent of today's working personnel managers scored so low on Civil Service exams, they did not qualify for employment with the United States Postal Service.

- Most personnel managers use interview time to make a list of "things to do" for the upcoming weekend.

- All personnel managers know exactly how hard it is to get a good job, hence the air of superiority that hangs over them.

- Approximately two-thirds of all personnel managers live alone and own at least two cats.

- Because of unlimited access to personnel files, many personnel managers enjoy a second income using strategic phone calls placed to fellow employees very late at night.

What does all this mean to you? The personnel manager is your first major obstacle between you and your dream job—you have seen the

Ever wonder what kind of notes personnel managers are making about you during interviews? Actually, most are just updating their "Things To Do" list!

enemy, and she or he is bitter, resentful, and unhappy at work, and lives a miserable social existence. Be careful with this person. He or she is highly volatile, holds your future in his or her hands, and—if you get hired—will have access to your personnel file. Take strides to get on this person's good side.

If you are lucky enough to find employment, the personnel manager will make sure you fill out your W-2 form, explain company policy, and describe your benefit package on your first day of work. After that, you need not worry about the personnel manager again and may avoid him or her just as your colleagues do. With any luck—and if you find work in a really big company—you may not even see the personnel manager again until the company is "unexpectedly forced to let you go."

SECTION TWO: INTERVIEWING

CHAPTER FOUR: PROPER INTERVIEW ATTIRE

"Dantony" (not his real name) decided to wear his lucky hat to an interview—he thought it would give him the confidence he needed to make a good impression. Unfortunately, the beer cans suspended on either side of his plastic chapeau went dry in the middle of the interview, and the

> **REMEMBER, IT'S A TIE, NOT A HANDKERCHIEF**

slurping sounds of both straws sucking air distracted the personnel manager. Sadly, Dantony didn't get the job.

Interviewers must decide among many applicants, so we must once again emphasize the importance of first impressions. Always look your best, but at the same time don't upstage your interviewer—there's no need to wear an Armani suit when interviewing for a job offering entry-level pay. Actually, as the story above illustrates, we have found it more important to consider what *not* to wear. What should you keep in the closet the next time you step out for a job? Use the proceeding advice as a guide.

GENERAL APPEARANCE TIPS

- While dyeing your hair is fine, try to stay within certain boundaries. Whatever color you choose should actually appear somewhere in nature, but steer clear of anything inspired by tropical fish or jungle aviary.

- Some job experts will tell you to wear a light fragrance; others say to avoid colognes altogether—there's just no telling what might offend an interviewer's olfactory sense. Whatever you decide, we do know that most interviewers have a poor initial reaction to any scent featuring pine cleaner.

- Outside of a nice tan, it's always best to maintain your natural skin color.

- If you must wear tinted contacts, take strides to ensure both are of the same color. If a mix-up occurs, it is probably best to admit your mistake. It turns out that most interviewers understand simple human error better than a claim to be part Shetland sheepdog.

- Remember, hygienic care should take place prior to the interview. If, however, you must clean your glasses, do not use clothing. Employers often seem inconvenienced when forced to retuck their shirt or blouse.

No matter how proud of your heritage, you probably shouldn't don ceremonial garb for an interview.

Proper Interview Clothes

They say clothes make the man. While we have no idea what that means, let alone who "they" are or what they think makes the woman, we do acknowledge the importance of wearing appropriate business attire to interviews. So save that little backless number for cocktail parties and don't try dusting off that old tux you wore to the prom (no matter how good you look in powder blue, and especially if you went to high school in the '70s). Refer to the following lists when picking out your interview ensemble.

Patterns to Steer Clear Of

- Anything featuring the "Peanuts" gang.

- Plaid (unless, of course, you are of Scottish descent. Even then, only wear the family tartan and remember, lads, to keep your knees together!).

- Anything popularized by country music of the 1990s (if Garth Brooks or one of the Judds wore it on an album cover, keep it in your closet).

- Paisley.

- Anything resembling your great aunt's curtains or couch throws.

Fabrics to Avoid

- Spandex, Latex, or any other petroleum-based fabric.

- Velcro.

- Polyester. (Disregard if you're up for a job in auto sales. Remember: no upstaging!)

- Hemp.

- Chain mail (unless presented in an extremely tasteful manner).

Neckwear Tips

- Don't wear any ties that require batteries.

- Avoid neckwear purchased at Wall Drug, Graceland, or any of the fine establishments in Branson, Missouri.

- If you must wear a bolo, steer clear of anything made from turquoise and Black Hills gold, particularly those items shaped like a state.

- Remember: it's a tie, not a handkerchief.

- Finally, never, ever, pull at your tie when you get nervous. One little tug and even the best clips pop right off.

FOOTWEAR

- Proper footwear is important. Obviously, sneakers are inappropriate for most interviews. Some personnel managers examine shoes closely because many how-to-interview books claim that shoes reflect the job candidate. Consequently, make sure your shoes are polished and in good condition. We've also found it important to remove the "L" and "R" from their tops prior to an interview but *after* you have put them on. We learned the hard way, but no matter how nice they look, shoes should always be worn on the correct foot.

CHAPTER FIVE:
THE INTERVIEW

We've been on many, many, oh so many interviews. We've analyzed a variety of our confrontations with personnel managers, examined our responses as well as those of our interviewers and any peace officers present. We already knew that behaving professionally and answering questions in a straightforward, articulate manner are as important as

> **DON'T INTERRUPT BY SHOUTING, "OKAY, OKAY—MY TURN!"**

how you look—that's common sense. But we have now pinpointed the exact things said and done in past interviews that may have damaged our opportunities, and developed that data into the advice in this chapter. We hope it helps.

POOR INTERVIEW RESPONSES

While it is generally considered good to be yourself and to be as honest as possible, you should be cautious. We have found that, in fact, being "yourself" may present problems. Below we provide a list of answers and actions we have found to be inappropriate in the eyes of most interviewers.

- The first few moments of an interview can be awkward. Self-discipline is important. Try to repress any natural inclination to begin with "Knock-knock...."

- The personnel manager will generally begin the interview. If, however, you wish to show you're a self-starter by initiating the process yourself, avoid little "ice breakers" such as replacing the handshake by giving the interviewer "nuggies" or by sneaking up behind the interviewer, covering his or her eyes with your hands, and saying "Guess who?"

- Always rely on your medical records as a sufficient account of past surgeries. There is really no need to show your scars.

Biting nails is inadvisable: there's no reason an interviewer's hands should be anywhere near your mouth.

- If you must interject to clarify a previous statement, don't interrupt your interviewer by beginning a sentence with "Okay, okay— my turn!"

- Biting nails is also inadvisable. Some consider it to be "unclean" or to demonstrate nervousness. Really, there is no reason to bring the interviewer's hand(s) anywhere near your mouth.

- If you suffer from a cold or hay fever at the time of the interview, it is perfectly natural for you to occasionally stop and blow your nose. If you must, do so without comment.

- While, of course, you'll want your prospective employer to see you as multitalented, avoid displaying the old armpit noise trick or trying to say the entire alphabet while belching (if you are nervous, you will inevitably have trouble when you reach "W").

- Along that same line, remember that everybody can do an impression of John Wayne and Ed Sullivan.

- We have also found that most personnel managers are unimpressed with mime. The old "Trapped-in-a-box" and "Walking-against-the-wind" routines have become interview clichés.

- Fumbling or stumbling over words is an inevitable nervous reaction during the interviewing process. Just do your best. Avoid blaming any weak responses on a canker sore.

- Keep all presentations of vacation slides as brief as possible.

- In today's workplace, presenting yourself as environmentally conscious is important. However, avoid illustrating your stance by sorting the interviewer's garbage.

You may be proud that you haven't heard those little voices for a while, but not all personnel managers consider that a "positive trait."

ANSWERING THE "TWO BIG QUESTIONS"

The interview will eventually reach a point when the personnel manager runs out of questions pertaining to your educational background and related employment experience. At this time, most unimaginative interviewers fall back on two traditional questions found in most how-to-interview books: 1) "Name three of your positive traits" and 2) "Name three of your negative traits." While, again, it is always best to be honest, some replies elicit a negative response (ranging, we have discovered, from a simple rolling of the eyes to a phone call to security). To ensure your interview isn't cut short, avoid using the following responses.

UNIMPRESSIVE POSITIVE TRAITS:

- You still have all your own teeth.

- You finally found just the right balance of medications and haven't heard those "little voices" in almost two months.

- You have been a guest on "Geraldo" during sweeps week—three times!

- You have an ability to somehow look busy whenever the boss is around.
- You have every episode of "Gilligan's Island" on videocassette.

UNIMPRESSIVE NEGATIVE TRAITS:

- You have an uncontrollable impulse to remove all the "do not remove this tag" tags from mattresses and furniture.
- You still haven't recovered emotionally from the untimely breakup of Tony Orlando and Dawn.
- You fear that many corporate supervisors are actually space aliens who have infiltrated society and are just waiting for the signal to begin taking over the world.
- You seem to have lost your knack for finding garage sales.
- You don't quite have all the episodes of "Gilligan's Island" on videocassette (this response may indicate that you can't program your VCR).

WATCH OUT FOR TRICK QUESTIONS!

A common question personnel managers often ask is "What did you take with you from your last job?" Careful! This is a trick question. They are looking for answers like "knowledge" or "experience." However you choose to respond, do not say, "A big ol' box of office supplies."

ASKING QUESTIONS

After answering questions, you will naturally want to ask some of your own. Many potential employees often ask about salary, benefits, etc. Interviewers expect you to have some questions. There are, however, some questions you should *not* ask at this time. Use the following as a guide:

- "How much vacation time can I use before I start?"

- "I don't suppose I could get an advance on, say, my first year's salary?"

- "How do you folks feel about bare feet?"

- "Could we work it so I can take my breaks while 'All My Children' is on?"

- "You don't have any of those . . . security cameras, do you?"

- "Are pets welcome?"

A SPECIAL NOTE FOR THE GUYS:

While it's perfectly fine to compliment the personnel manager on the "handsome family" in the requisite desk photograph, we have found it inappropriate at this time to ask if the teenage daughter is allowed to date "older men."

You can safely assume that you won't be called upon to display any "special skills" during most interviews.

INTERVIEW TIME KILLERS

You'll want to fill that awkward gap in the interview while the personnel manager checks with your parole officer or verifies an entry on your résumé with the company psychologist. While it's always good to appear busy, avoid participating in the following activities while biding your time:

- Playing with your Game Boy.

- Flossing.

- Flipping through the personnel manager's Rolodex.

- Practicing yoga and/or meditation.

- Cleaning your pistol.

- Removing stitches.

- Watering plants.

- Practicing bird calls.

- Napping.

- Playing with your "Game Boy" (if you know what we mean …).

IN CASE OF INTERVIEW EMERGENCY

No matter how well prepared and confident you are walking into an interview, things may not always go your way. We have, for instance, found ourselves caught off guard by questions that interrupt perfectly good daydreams. You can take several courses of action to remedy these moments, but you may panic if the going really gets tough. Be careful not to make the same mistakes we have:

- Never perform the Heimlich maneuver on anyone who is not actually choking.

- Don't pretend to have suddenly gone blind. (Unless, of course, the interview is going absolutely miserably.)

- Likewise, feigning a *grand mal* seizure is also a poor idea. You may fool the interviewer, but the paramedics will see straight through your ruse.

- We also do not advise excusing yourself to go to the rest room and then returning to blame all your earlier responses on "Raul," your evil twin. This seldom fools anyone. (If you really must resort to this method, changing ties in the bathroom helps).

- No matter how much you panic, by all means control your hemorrhaging!

No matter how bad the interview's going, never give the Heimlich maneuver to anyone who isn't actually choking.

CHAPTER SIX: THE LUNCHEON INTERVIEW

Invited out to lunch to talk over an employment opportunity? Great! A lunch interview is a very positive sign. You not only have an opportunity to impress a potential employer, but you also scam a free meal!

A lunch interview usually also means that a prospective employer is seriously considering hiring you and believes you have opportunities for positions elsewhere. It's their way of trying to impress you (imagine that!). It indi-

> **THAT'S**
> **_NOT_**
> **LEMON SOUP.**

cates they have already put you on the short list and that only a major screwup could stop you from getting the job. Either that or the personnel manager's favorite restaurant is offering a special on fish. Make sure, however, to follow the advice outlined below.

MINDING YOUR LUNCH INTERVIEW MANNERS

Some interviewers will watch you carefully during a luncheon interview, looking for character traits that could make or break your application. For instance, if you salt your food before you taste it, this action could be interpreted as reflective of your decision-making process. We have found the same applies to ketchup, particularly in ethnic restaurants. Also keep the following rules of thumb in mind:

- Avoid any action that immediately follows the imperative "Watch this!"

- That's *not* lemon soup.

- Do not make airplane noises as you bring your fork to your mouth.

- Although it's not nearly as efficient, place your napkin in your lap instead of tucking it into your collar.

- Vichyssoise is *supposed* to be cold.

- Even if you're not sure which fork to use, don't simply ignore the tined utensils. Even using the wrong fork, we now know, is preferable to using your hands.

- If it's the restaurant's custom to offer your table a complimentary bread basket, don't shout out, "Dibs on the Melba toast!" You can always just ask for extra.

Even if you're not sure which tined utensil is correct, always use a fork (yes, even with chicken).

PROPER LUNCH INTERVIEW CONVERSATION

No matter what the topic of conversation may be, you will *not* want to use the following terms during the restaurant interview:

- Holding tank (or anything else referring to septic systems).

- Regularity.

- Cadaver.

- Hair ball.

- Soy.

- Spork.

- Gingivitis.

- Anthrax.

- Meat loaf
  (in reference to the food).

- Meat Loaf
  (in reference to the entertainer).

- Anything in reference to Ernest Borgnine's back (see also "Hair ball").

You may also wish to avoid using the following phrases:

- "You gonna finish that?"

- "That doesn't look like gristle."

- "God, I hope they validate."

- "Are those clams? You know what I saw on 'Sixty Minutes' about clams?"

- "Wow, it's been a while since I've been able to keep pork down this long."

LUNCHEON INTERVIEW BONUS TIP!

While your waitperson will inevitably ask if he or she can bring you a cocktail, it is not always in your best interest to imbibe spirits during an interview, no matter how nervous you are. You don't want the interviewer to think you have a "problem." Your best bet is to let the personnel manager reply first, and then follow his or her lead. In any case, employ moderation and always keep in mind that the waitperson's offer is not necessarily a come-on.

WHEN THE BILL COMES

You can safely assume that if you are being interviewed in a restaurant, the company will pick up the tab. So, when the bill arrives, there is no need to search your suit coat or purse pretending to have lost your wallet. Also, leave the bill on the table. Do not, as we have learned, pick it up and shout out "Whoa! What'd we do—break somethin'?"

CHAPTER SEVEN: THE TELEPHONE INTERVIEW

Confused by the idea of a telephone interview? Don't be. Remember, personnel managers are a lazy lot who receive many applications for each position they must fill. To make things easier on themselves, they sometimes screen applicants by phone. Most interview guides will tell you to treat this process with professionalism. Some even suggest wearing clothes even though the personnel manager can't even see you! While professionalism is important, we have discovered many potential dangers involved in this seemingly innocent procedure. Use the advice on the following pages as a guide.

> **ALWAYS HANG UP *BEFORE* YOU FLUSH.**

Phone Interview Call Waiting Etiquette

Nothing annoys a personnel manager more than having a phone interview interrupted by a "call waiting" call to your phone. If a call does break in, try turning it to your advantage: "Sorry about that. IBM again. They're pressuring me to accept a position, but I told them I'm waiting for you to make an offer." (Don't, however, use this when the phone interview is actually with Big Blue. Believe us, they don't appreciate it a bit.) If bluffing doesn't work, apologize like mad and make something else up. Whatever you do, avoid the following excuses:

- "Just my parole officer—looks like I'm a few days late calling in. Picky, picky."

- "My mom's attorney again—boy, say a few things on 'Sally Jesse' and everyone thinks they can judge you."

- "Stupid telemarketers—I keep telling them I have all the marital aids I need for now."

- "My old boss—how am I supposed to know about all those long-distance calls?"

- "Sorry, that was the clinic verifying my appointment. It's about time, too. I can't even sit down."

PHONE INTERVIEW PHRASES TO AVOID

- "Do you accept VISA?"

- "What number did you dial?"

- "It's your dime!"

- "If it's not delivered in thirty minutes, is it free?"

- "What are you wearing?"

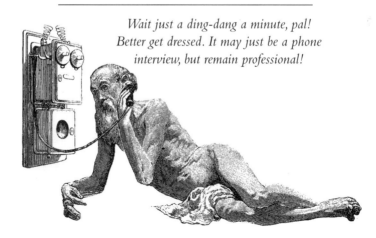

Wait just a ding-dang a minute, pal! Better get dressed. It may just be a phone interview, but remain professional!

General Phone Interview Tips

- It is not necessary to describe yourself physically.

- You don't need a major credit card handy (see also "Phrases to Avoid," above).

- Hang up *before* you flush.

- In the tub? Keep splashing to a minimum and try not to squeak any rubber bath-time friends.

- Finally, try to schedule the interview so it doesn't conflict with other important activities (especially if you don't have one of those easy-to-program VCRs).

In Case of Emergency

If you sense things are really turning against you, try feigning line interference. Make static noises and hold the receiver away from your mouth and say (interjecting with more "static" at the ellipses): "What did ... can't seem to ... flash of lightning, and then ... some kind of inter- ... breaking up ... hear you ... will call back ..."

Been on hold long enough to catch Phil AND Oprah? Your phone interview may not be going as smoothly as you think.

Finally, unplug your telephone and take some time to regain your composure.

How can you tell if things aren't going your way? Look for the following warning signs:

- Long, awkward pauses.

- Snoring (by either the interviewer or yourself).

- You hear other voices and giggling and sus- pect you've been put on "speaker."

- You've been on hold long enough to catch both Phil and Oprah.

- You suspect the interviewer may be lying about "line interference."

Section Three:
After the Interview

Chapter Eight:
The Follow-up Letter

If you're anything like us, you'd like to think that a job search ends after the trauma of the interview, and that you can relax, watch TV, and wait for your postal carrier to bring your rejection letter and unemployment check. Many applicants, however, choose to follow their interviews with a brief letter to the personnel manager thanking him or her for the opportunity.

> **Avoid addressing the personnel manager as "Bubbles."**

Most employment guides suggest mentioning some aspect of the interview you thought went particularly well or a topic that matched your strengths with those the company is seeking. However, the follow-up letter also provides another opportunity for you to goof up your application. The elementary principles for the follow-up letter are similar to those for the cover letter, so follow the same basic guidelines concerning matters of style and avoiding bad starts outlined in Chapter Two.

Also, remember that simply because you have spent time with the personnel manager, you are not necessarily on a first-name basis. Even if you are, try to maintain formality. Whatever the case, avoid addressing the personnel manager as "Bubbles," "Fats," and any other nickname or term of endearment.

POORLY WRITTEN FOLLOW-UP LETTERS

We wrote the letters on the following pages long before we knew what *not* to include in a successful follow-up letter. Again, the names of the companies have been changed to give us a better chance to get a job. Study our errors and avoid them in your own letters.

POORLY WRITTEN FOLLOW-UP LETTER #1

1 January 1996

Personnel Manager
Acme Promotions
Anytown, U.S.A.

Mr. Interviewer:

I enjoyed meeting with you last Thursday to discuss the opening for a fiscal budget director.

Please understand that I thought you said "physical." That should explain the dancers.

Again, sorry about the mess. I'd have been more than happy to have mopped that up for you.

Sincerely,

Danny Y.

DID YOU SPOT THE MISTAKE?

Our letter addresses a low point of the interview. Keep your correspondence upbeat and play up your strengths! Don't remind interviewers of unfortunate incidents they may have already forgotten.

Now, see if you can find our failure in letter #2.

POORLY WRITTEN FOLLOW-UP LETTER #2

1 January 1996

Personnel Manager
Acme University
Anytown, U.S.A.

Ms. Interviewer:

I enjoyed meeting with you last Thursday to discuss the women's studies teaching position at Acme.

Concerning our disagreement over your wife's photo: It turns out you are right: Roxy Goldbloom, not your lovely Mrs., was the June 1987 Pet of the Month.

I stand corrected and apologize if this caused any inconvenience.

Sincerely,

Tony X.

DID YOU SPOT THE MISTAKE?

Note that the letter refers to the interviewer's wife, yet it is addressed to "Ms. Interviewer." This may be a simple typo on our part, but mistaken gender issues—although common—can be very upsetting to some personnel managers. Again: Proofread! Proofread! Proofread!

Up for another challenge? Try letter #3.

POORLY WRITTEN FOLLOW-UP LETTER #3

1 January 1996

Personnel Manager
Acme Incorporated
Anytown, U.S.A.

Ms. Interviewer:

I want to thank you again for the opportunity to meet with you to discuss a potential working relationship with Acme, Inc.

I walked away pleased with our meeting and hope to join the ranks at your wonderful company.

Gotta go—Oprah's on!

Sincerely,

Danny Y.

DID YOU SPOT THE MISTAKE?

The informal "Gotta" might work during a conversation between friends or in scripted dialogue to indicate a fictional character's unique pronunciation, but it has no place in a formal business letter. The sentence should have read: "I must now take my leave—it seems Ms. Winfrey's television program is about to begin."

Too easy? Try letter #4!

POORLY WRITTEN FOLLOW-UP LETTER #4

1 January 1996

Personnel Manager
Acme Manufacturing
Anytown, U.S.A.

Mr. Interviewer:

I'd like to express my sincere gratitude for the opportunity to interview for the Safety Inspector position with Acme.

Again, sorry about any confusion or work delays I may have caused. It is comforting, however, to know that your fire alarms are very accessible.

Sincerely,

Tony X.

Did you spot the mistake?

While "safety inspector" may be a job title, it is not an official title of a dignitary placed in front of a name (i.e. "President Quayle")—no need to capitalize!

Did we fool ya? In any case, you have one more opportunity to spot the mistake!

POORLY WRITTEN FOLLOW-UP LETTER #5

1 January 1996

Personnel Manager
Acme Marketing
Anytown, U.S.A.

Ms. Interviewer:

Thanks for the opportunity to discuss the opening with Acme's public relations department.

Please note that I can no longer be reached at the phone number listed on my résumé. However, if you look out your office window—now, for instance—you'll see an orange and red van. That's me!

Sincerely,

Danny Y.

DID YOU SPOT THE MISTAKE?

We haven't!

CHAPTER NINE:
INTERPRETING REJECTION LETTERS

Feeling bad about receiving a rejection letter? Don't. We've learned that personnel managers are a lot like some women in our lives: they run from us because of their own problems, not because we wouldn't make perfectly good husbands or employees.

And even after all the wisdom gained on our long quest for gainful employment, we still find ourselves at the receiving end of rejection letters. You should expect to find similar correspondence gracing your mailbox as you fine-tune your job-search skills. But have hope! Sure, we're still unemployed, but we're both happily married to wonderfully patient women.

> **CHANGING YOUR ADDRESS MAY BE THE ONLY WAY TO AVOID REJECTION LETTERS.**

The important thing to remember at this point is to never accept what a rejection letter says at face value. You must interpret the subtext to get the true meaning of the message. Only then will you be able to apply what you learn to your next cover letter, résumé, or interview.

To help you learn to interpret the hidden messages of the personnel manager's pen, we have deciphered actual rejection letters we have received over the years. On the following page is a copy of a rejection letter one of us received in response to a cover letter and résumé he sent as an initial position query.

ACTUAL INITIAL QUERY
REJECTION LETTER

2 January 1996

Danny Y.
c/o the East End Y.M.C.A.
Anytown, U.S.A.

Dear Applicant:

Thank you for your interest in the recent opening here at Acme Inc.

We received many applications from highly qualified people such as yourself. Through a difficult selection process, we have filled the position and are no longer considering applications.

Please feel welcome to apply again should another position open matching your qualifications.

Sincerely,

Bob Johnson

SAME LETTER, INTERPRETED LINE BY LINE:

- Dear Applicant (*not bothering to even type in applicant's name*) =

  "I'll never actually have to meet you, so why should I bother taking the effort to address you as an individual?"

- Thank you for your interest in our recent opening here at Acme Inc. =

  "Thank you for generally wasting my time and adding to the enormous stack of queries from other unqualified applicants for some job I won't bother to address specifically; this is, after all, a form letter."

- We received many applications from highly qualified people such as yourself. =

  "We got a lot of résumés that looked just like yours: a liberal arts degree and no relevant work experience."

- Through a difficult selection process, we have filled the position and are no longer considering applications. =

"After tossing out the résumés of you and all the other liberal arts majors, we had two qualified applicants, one of whom never served time for a felony. We hired her and enjoyed a chuckle or two as we shredded the other résumés."

- Please feel welcome to apply again should another position open matching your qualifications. =

"Don't bother us again unless we have an opening for an espresso machine operator who can't even handle the simple-minded procedures involved in retail sales."

- Sincerely, =

"Sincerely" is the personnel manager's feeble attempt at using irony.

Pretty grim, don't you think? Well, if you think that's bad, the next page shows a copy of a rejection letter one of us received following an interview.

ACTUAL POST-INTERVIEW REJECTION LETTER

2 January 1996

Tony X.
501 N. 12th Avenue East
Anytown, U.S.A.

Dear Mr. X:

I enjoyed our meeting concerning the recent opening in our firm. You made quite an impression.

Although your qualifications are unique, we can only hire one person to fill this position. Unfortunately, your application was not accepted.

I will keep your file on record should we have another opportunity for someone with your qualifications.

I wish you good fortune in your search for employment.

Best Regards,

Bob Johnson

SAME LETTER, INTERPRETED LINE BY LINE:

- Dear Mr. X: (*use of actual name instead of just "applicant"*) =

  "We hired a temp to create a data base of those we interviewed and used a computer mail merge feature to make it look like we really considered your application."

- I enjoyed our meeting concerning the recent opening in our firm. =

  "I laughed out loud sharing your responses with colleagues after you interviewed for some job I won't bother to address specifically; this is, after all, a form letter."

- You made quite an impression. =

  "I vaguely recall your unfortunate choice of apparel."

- Although your qualifications are unique ... =

  "Not very many applicants minored in both Chippewa and medieval architecture; however…"

- …we can only hire one person to fill this position. =

  "…the owner's nephew needed a job—and he got it."

- Unfortunately, your application was not accepted. =

  "You didn't seriously expect us to hire you for this position, did you?"

- I will keep your file on record should we have another opportunity for someone with your qualifications. =

  "I'll try to think of your name if we ever need someone to do some heavy lifting; in the meantime, we're keeping your résumé in the 'circular file.'"

- I wish you good fortune in your search for employment. =

  "Good luck finding a job that doesn't somehow involve a deep fryer."

- Best regards, =

  The interviewer is employing sarcasm.

We hope that, by sharing our mistakes, we have helped to make your job search easier. Good luck, but remember it's a long, hard road and not many qualified individuals ever find a job in their chosen career fields.

Don't let that bother you, and don't worry if you have trouble finding work.

> # DON'T
> ## DESPAIR.

Remember, soon you'll be an angry, bitter person with an undergraduate degree in the liberal arts and no practical experience—a person whose lack of money has eliminated social interaction and left you willing to do anything, no matter how low or degrading, for money. You are grooming yourself for a career in the glamorous world of human resources. Soon you'll be a fully qualified personnel manager!

THESE BAD DOG APPAREL ITEMS SHOW YOU HAVE:
A. A great sense of humor
B. Great taste in humor books
C. A limited wardrobe budget
D. A limited wardrobe
E. All of the above

BONUS HINT:
Don't wear these quality shirts to your next interview!

WILL EAT FOR FOOD *tee* #PAR001

I'M WITH STUPID *tee* #PAR002

100% MONEY-BACK QUALITY GUARANTEE

COOL BAD DOG STUFF
Your life won't be complete without these quality BAD DOG items.*
*Completeness of individual lives may vary

BAD DOG MUG
#BD003

SAVE HUGE BUCKS ON A LITTER OF FOUR BAD DOG MUGS #BD004

Back of mug says:

I ♥ MY BAD DOG

Cap Back Design

BAD DOG CAP
#BD002

BAD DOG LOGO *Sweat* #BD001S
BAD DOG LOGO *T-Shirt* #BD001T

ORDERING INFORMATION

You can order by mail* or phone.
Fill out this handy order form prior
to calling so you don't forget anything.

TM

_____ Will Eat for Food T-Shirt *(PAR001)* $17.95
_____ I'm With Stupid T-Shirt *(RCS002)* $17.95

_____ Bad Dog Logo T-Shirt *(BD001T)* $17.95
_____ Bad Dog Logo Sweat *(BD001S)* $27.95
_____ Bad Dog Embroidered Cap *(BD002)* $19.95
_____ Bad Dog Mug *(BD003)* $8.95
_____ Set of 4 Bad Dog Mugs *(BD004)* $25.00

XXL size t-shirts and sweats add $1.50
MN residents add 6.5% tax on non-apparel items
Allow two to three weeks for delivery
Shipping/handling charges: $5.00

Pick One:
☐ Free Button
☐ Free
   Bumper
   Sticker

FREE BUTTON | **Sub Total Items** $ _____
OR BUMPER | **Tax** $ _____
STICKER | **Shipping Charges** $ _$5.00_
WITH | **Total** $ _____
EVERY
ORDER

BAD DOG TOLL-FREE ORDER LINE
1-800-270-5863   VISA MasterCard

* To order by mail send your order with your name, address, phone
  with a check or money order to:
  Bad Dog Press P.O. Box 130066 Roseville, MN 55113

DO YOUR BAD DOG SHOPPING ON-LINE:
http://www.octane.com

BITE INTO THESE OTHER

BAD DOG™ BOOKS

They call when you're in the tub. They call during dinner. They call when you're "reading" in the bathroom. And whenever they call, they try to sell you something you more than likely don't want.

They're telemarketers, and Bad Dog Press's latest offering—*How to Get Rid of a Telemarketer*—presents dozens of hilarious ways to help readers regain precious spare time free of senseless solicitation and leave even the most tenacious telemarketers speechless.

Has your soul had enough chicken soup to make you gag? The souls at Bad Dog Press sure have, so to cleanse America's palate they're offering *Rubber Chickens for the Soul*, a parody of the popular, inspiration-laden *Chicken Soup for the Soul* books.

While the stories in Rubber Chickens may not exactly open the heart and rekindle the spirit like those in the "Chicken Soup" books, they'll at the very least rekindle your heartburn.

You know the type: they encourage mimes; they pass you on the highway and then drive too slow; they talk during movies; too often, they're your relatives. They're highly annoying people, and they play a much larger role in your life than do the highly effective.

Bad Dog's *The Habits of Seven Highly Annoying People* explores and exploits some of the most vexatious folks you'll ever meet. Great to give as an anonymous gift to people you find particularly annoying!

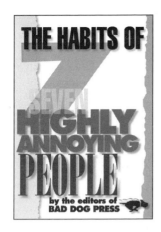

THE HABITS OF
SEVEN HIGHLY ANNOYING PEOPLE
by the editors of
BAD DOG PRESS

A WHOLE NEW BREED OF HUMOR BOOKS!

Like our namesakes, we at Bad Dog Press aren't afraid to dig in the trash, chew the furniture, or take off dragging the leash—but we do so with tasteful, funny books that will have you laughing all the way home from the bookstore.

As you read this, the folks at Bad Dog are busy preparing other books that you'll love! Watch your bookstore humor section for our latest releases.

HAVE A PEEK AT OUR FUTURE BOOKS!

Visit the BAD DOG Humor On-Line Web page to preview upcoming books, participate in fun contests, join in funny forums, and find out how you can contribute to future Bad Dog books.
http://www.octane.com